I Hope You Know

Words for Clarity and Purpose

Also by Barbara Gianquitto

4:04ᴀᴍ Thoughts

Awakening of the Heart

Mirrors of Time

I
Hope
You
Know

*Words for
Clarity and Purpose*

BARBARA GIANQUITTO

Editor: Stefanie Briar

ISBN 978-1-739 5880-7- 6

To those whose wisdom shaped my journey
whose lessons, like whispers in the wind,
guided my steps when the path was unclear.
I have gathered each moment
the joy and the struggle
the questions and the answers
and now I offer them here.
In these words I share what I have learned
for every experience was a teacher
and in embracing them, I have found my voice.

Author's Note

If I had to choose one word to define my journey, it would be "Serendipity." I have never believed that anything happens randomly. It might have taken me a moment, or even years to understand why something happened (or didn't happen as I wished).

I've had countless "a-ha!" moments and life lessons that left me speechless—a rare feat for an author. So, as all poets do, I wrote everything down, I created art, and gave life to poems and pieces of prose that are now just before you.

These poems aim to connect us through our shared humanity, the beauty and power of going back to the simple things: to compassion, to love, to hope; the ultimate way to reclaim ourselves whole.

This is a book of hope, a pause in the everyday chaos, a way to make you feel—hopefully—less alone in the world.

This book contains exactly 111 poems, all released into the world and the Universe on the date 11/11. The number sequence 111 is considered to be a master number in numerology, and it carries a powerful vibration aligned with spiritual growth and enlightenment. It is believed to be a message from your angels that you are connected to the divine and that you are on the right path.

Maybe this is your sign that you are meant to be reading this book at this exact moment, it could be the Universe's way of guiding you toward the insights and comfort you seek.

One thing I am sure of is that there is a message in this book for You, and You only.

Perhaps it will hold you when you can't hold yourself or give you the courage to let go of what no longer serves you. Maybe both. Whichever it is, I hope it finds you and - most importantly - I hope it stays with you.

Open your heart, turn the page. Let's begin.

Contents

I think we are all just here to love,
to be loved,
to bring some light into the darkness,
to welcome a new dawn,
to walk each other home.

From now on

I will speak a simple language
made of love and birds,
tenderness and courage,
mixed tapes and strawberry fields.

You'll find me here,
in every unspoken dream,
at the edge of time
waiting for the final dawn.

A tale for the brave,
a story for the lost:
no more duality,
no high or lows.

There is no negative
or positive:
I am You, and You are me.
We are made of love,
of compassion,
of truth.

I will speak a simple language

a language of the stars
written in the night sky,
guiding us through the darkness
with a light that never dies.

With every word unspoken,
with every touch unseen,
We'll weave a tapestry of life
in hues of gold and green.

So listen to the quiet,
feel your heart's steady beat.
For in this simple language,
our souls will always meet.

Star Seed

I began my journey in the explosion of a galaxy, some billions of years ago. I travelled far amongst constellations and galaxies, not yet known, in a place where the notion of time was *now* and the idea of space was *everywhere*.

You see, there is a reason why I feel homesick for the stars. It's because I was called upon this earth to share some of the light I was made of. There was never a reason for words where I came from. I guess that's why, in this embodied life on Earth, I am challenged to use them for change: or maybe to revert to what was and still is the only possible language: love.

I guess somewhere between the stars and Earth, we forget where we come from and how powerful we really are. Because, you see, the magic is not left with the stars. We carry it within us here on Earth. Finding a way for our human bodies to contain it, accept it, and learn how to use it can be a great challenge.

I am here to remind you of this: magic resides inside all of us, hiding in that voice we don't give enough attention to. That one we call "intuition" or "gut feeling" that we often suppress. We didn't come here to be powerless, we didn't come here to be invisible, we didn't come here to have our voice muffled.

I know I didn't. And I know you didn't either.

So, stop hiding beautiful ones. And be the light you were always meant to be.

ADDING VOICE TO TRUTH

Yes, it has been said before
by other poets, better writers,
famous people, more popular authors:
one, ten, hundreds, millions of times.

But let me ask you something:
does the truth stop being true
just because it has been said already?

When the sun rises each morning,
does its light lose its brilliance
because it has shone a thousand times before?
When a song of love is sung,
does it lose its sweetness
because its melody is familiar?

I won't stop writing, I won't hide away.
In the tapestry of voices, mine may be a thread,
but each thread weaves a part of the whole.

I'll join the chorus, I'll make it *stronger*:

for every voice adds depth,
every echo adds resonance,
every whisper, every shout,
merges into a symphony of human experience.

Join it with me.

Bring your voice, your truth.

Together we will create harmony:
a melody that rings true,
a song that celebrates the timeless,
the ever-new, ever-true essence of our words.

Your mission

Your mission is to walk on and wide awake,
        not just with your eyes but with your heart.

   To remember why you are here. To honour the contracts you made before you decided to return, before you were even born. To bring some of the stardust your soul was forged in and light the path for those who have not yet remembered. To love and be loved. To welcome a new dawn.

To walk each other home.

On Healing

There's no timeline for healing.
There's no "you should be over it by now".
Go at your own pace.
Allow yourself to feel everything that you need to feel,
whenever you need to.
It's okay if it hits you all over again.
It's okay if you thought you were over it but spent a day
in sadness.

The truth is: it hurts because it meant something to you.
And sometimes grief is the only remnant that you have left
of that connection.
It's what keeps them with you, the last piece of them you
have left.
So you hold onto it like a blanket to keep you warm
and use the memories as an old movie whose ending never
played.

Half healed, half haunted.

And if today is the day, it's okay.
Let it be.
Let it be.

It was the year

It was the year I decided I wouldn't cry over a man ever again:
I packed my bags along with the rest of the melancholy
and sadness still drenched in my clothes.

New walls around me, unfamiliar noises, and
a well known sense of determination.
I've done this before; he wasn't the first who broke my heart.

So I let the tears go wherever they wanted to,
some even packed their own bags that I carefully placed
next to the boxes labelled "new home".

They'll always have a place where they can live, just like
memories.
I don't fear them anymore: tears are cleansing
like a strong wind sweeping off the fog.

It was the year I proclaimed myself free:
of obligations,
of labels,
of expectations.

It was the year
I finally
found *myself*.

Purpose

Have you ever considered the possibility that your sole mission in this life is to break generational trauma? To be the parent you didn't have? To pick up your kids from school, offer them your presence, sit down with them, do homework, make dinner? To do the mundane, magical tasks that seem menial but are monumental?

Have you ever considered the possibility that what you perceive as a lack of professional progress is actually a gift wrapped in kids' smiles and time spent with them?

What you're doing here is shaping future adults into the best version of themselves so they may grow strong and empowered. When their time comes to take their rightful place in this world, they won't have to battle with demons and anxiety like you have.

You're paving the way for a future generation that this world desperately needs. Keep moving forward without looking back. What you're doing is the most important job of all.

LOVE AND GRIEF

When grief comes, don't push it away.
When it sneaks in like a robber and gets inside your ribcage,
the very moment your heart is smiling for the first time
in a while,
don't push it away.

Open the door, pave the path,
build the road along the veins and arteries,
let it pass through your body.
Observe it, wave at it.
Don't trap it in this new love you are feeling.

Condense it in these sudden tears that are falling,
and as they drop, don't wipe them away.
Allow them to drop deep into the ground:
return to earth.

Release it
and then
let
    it
      go.

In the quiet moments, listen to what grief has to say,
and let love be the answer.

I HOPE, I TRULY DO

I hope this is the year you get to free yourself of the belief that you are not worthy. Of the chains that are keeping you from dreaming beyond your wildest dreams.

I hope you'll start to see how every fall has given you the strength to get back up again. How every tear has led you to more wisdom. How pain has been necessary to make that leap.

Don't stop now. Dare to dream in colours. Dare to ask life to show you how good it gets.

I hope this is the year that you can open your bruised heart to what's waiting for you behind the gates of pain, above the hills of doubt, on the other side of the door of fear.

Let go of anything and anyone that is not holding every other door wide open for you.

THE CIRCLE OF LIFE

People will come and go from our lives,
this is inevitable and almost *never*
about something we have done.

People drift away, values change.
Perspectives, interests,
and illnesses take centre stage

and sweep our loved ones away.
Life happens. The only guarantee is
that it *always* changes.

As *life evolves*, so do we.
So be gentle with yourself.
If you do nothing else at all today,

please do at least that.

Gratitude

Maybe you don't have to win today.
Maybe today you need to cheer others on from the sidelines.
Maybe today all your energy goes into smiling,
like really smiling for others' successes.

There is space for everyone, there must be;
you are me, and I am you, and we are all c-o-n-n-e-c-t-e-d.
When one wins, we all win.
Maybe today we delight in the role of supporter,

because without it there can't be any winner.
Take a breath and enjoy the view;
soak in the energy that is coming to you.
Celebrating others is the most loving thing you can do.

You look like someone who has survived
the biggest storms and toughest battles.
Yet, you are still smiling, you are still standing,
you are still living, you are still l o v i n g.
How magnificent is this?

When I go

When I go, please know that I have come home.
My place on Earth, in the house that you have shared with me,
was a momentary journey for my soul.
I have lived on Earth to meet you, to love you,
to teach you, to learn from you, to raise you, to lean on you.
I have come here to be your friend, your lover,
your mother, your daughter, your sister.
We were always meant to walk together.
We were never meant to do this forever.

I have come home to our ancestors.
I am again with the stars, where I was originally from.
Everything is calm here, and there is only love.
Everything is finally clear.

I want you to know that I am at peace,
and I want you to be at peace, too.
I know you will grieve me,
like I have grieved so many losses on Earth.
But this is not a true loss.
Because we are all one, and we can never be separated.
We are only in different dimensions right now.
Please believe me and find comfort
in knowing that nothing happened by chance.
Not one single moment, not one single bout of laughter,
not one single tear we shared together.
It was all meant to unfold this way.

So remember me with joy once the pain starts to subside.
I am a part of you as you were a part of me,
and I mean this literally.
We are all children of the Universe, made of the same stardust,
connected in ways we cannot comprehend,
fused together by love in every dimension,
in every timeline, in every reality.

Ever interwoven, ever unchanged.

The Mountain

Be as still as the mountain when the wind
       comes gushing down.
You don't have to stop the storm, you just have to weather it.
       Take a break, slow down.
Breathe in flow with the waves: rise and fall.
       The world won't stop turning, but the winds will.
The entire universe will wait, like the ground waits
       for the roots to sink deeper, like the moon waits
for the sun, like the rooster waits for the dawn,
       the world will wait for you.
And when you are ready, breathe in the victory.
       You haven't just survived,
you have given yourself permission to *grow*.

The Promise

I left my hair undone for a week
natural curls flowing in an unruly way:
the way I want to live my life,
the way you find me more Italian than ever.

You call me medusa and we laugh,
an unfamiliar sound in my throat
that I'm learning to welcome more and more each day.

Happiness has knocked on my door,
and - this time - I have answered.

And I'm taken aback at how beautiful you are
when you smile and forget all the things
you don't like about yourself.

If you could only see yourself the way I see you,
the way I feel you,
the way I believe I belong with you,
you'd never question this life ever again.

I stop to write a poem, or a sequence of words.
Who really cares what I'm writing?
I have time, the sun is shining on all my buried shadows.

And as you beg my chaos away
- in between fearing it and despising it -
 you love me harder.

And this, this is just another one
of the million reasons why I love you.
Right here, right now, in the silence
of the promise of everything.

Narrative

There's a point in life when,
if we take a big and long step back,
we get to change that narrative.
We get to see that growth is a gift, if we embrace it.
We get to reframe old beliefs and understand
that something might be happening
FOR us, rather than TO us.
Taking accountability for our own growth is growth itself.

Facing ourselves, (the real mess that is behind all the masks)
and saying, "You know what? I love you exactly as you are."
That's liberating.
It's difficult. It's terrifying.
But ultimately, it's incredibly empowering.

WHEN THEY COME BACK

When they come back
(because they will),
don't forget how they left.
How quickly they closed the door without a second thought.
Don't forget how you struggled to get back up
curled into a ball of tears on your kitchen floor.

When they come back
(because they will),
remember how they never gave you any explanation.
How you were imploring the gods for the pain to stop.
How your breath was stuck in every cell of your body
and even exhaling was painful.

When they come back
(because they will),
you will be well on your healing journey.
Use that strength to choose yourself, for once.

Please don't choose from your wound.
Choose from a newfound place of self-worth.

When they come back
(because they will),
wish them well.
Cry one last time if you must.
And then,
reclaim yourself
                    Free.

Safety

Return to yourself,
to your breath,
to everything that is pure and real.

Here, you are whole,
complete in your imperfections,
perfect in your uniqueness.

In this sacred space,
you are your own protector,
your own healer,
your own sanctuary.

In the stillness, hear the whisper of your soul,
a guiding voice leading you back to peace.
Feel the ground beneath you, solid and supportive,
rooting you in the present moment.

Return to yourself,
to your breath,
to everything that is pure and real.

Return to the safety of your own arms.

Lean in

When everything feels like breaking,
lean into love, compassion, and kindness:

towards yourself first and foremost.

Love yourself endlessly, with all you have to give.
Show the world you deserve to be loved unconditionally.

Everything, EVERYTHING, will follow.

At our core, love is all we know.

Power

Moving away from negativity and toxicity
is most powerful when done in total silence.

You don't need the last conversation.
You don't need them to validate your pain for it to be real,
and certainly, you don't need them to fix what they broke.

Move away in silence,
with purpose,
and in power.

The Past

It's so easy to go back to where the chaos feels most familiar.

But the road to balance often requires leaving your comfort zone.

Move towards new and unfamiliar chaos, the excitement of unexplored territories.

The past rarely has something new to say.

ORIGAMI

I've spent my life shrinking
into other people's view of the world, of me,
trying to fit into the smallest origami box
just because I thought that was

the safest place:
unseen, unheard.

What I finally realised is that
just because they didn't see my worth,
it didn't mean I was unworthy.

Don't make yourself smaller
just because they can't contain
your infinite magnificence,
beautiful soul.

TRUTH

Speak your truth, out loud:
the raw, unfiltered, gut-wrenching truth.
Even when it falls on deaf ears, use your voice.

You deserve to be heard and seen.
When you are at your lowest,
when you are at your highest.

When your needs are not being met
and you want to address it, speak your truth.
Live in alignment with your purpose and highest self.

Don't hold it inside any longer.
Reclaim yourself; the world needs more of this.
The world needs more of you.

It is really quite simple:
If it doesn't open, it isn't your door.

ANTITHESIS

Love and grief are not the antithesis of one another.

There is space for everything if you allow yourself
to feel *everything* that is coming up to the fullest.

Grieving the past and working on old traumas doesn't have
to stop us from experiencing love.

Accept and acknowledge that we are human beings, that
healing is never linear,
and that we are always a work in progress when it comes
to healing our traumas.

It is okay to grieve and love at the same time.

EVERYTHING HAPPENS FOR A REASON

And sometimes the reason
is that we just needed to let them go.

Say no.
Step a w a y.

   Don't engage in chaos.
        Your feelings and reactions
                are absolutely v a l i d.

GROWTH

The moments of growth
are the most unsettling, even painful.
It feels like you are lost,
ungrounded, with no clarity.
The new direction is only hidden
in the fog that surrounds you.
I know it's scary to trust the process,
but stay with it.

Selfies

I perfected the art of taking selfies, I think.

How to tilt my face towards the light so that my under eyes bags don't show as much, to get the impression I don't have all these wrinkles and how - for the life of me - I can't find a good concealer that doesn't settle into my fine lines.

I perfected the art of taking selfies.

How to part my hair in such a way that my grey hair doesn't show until the next hair appointment. Somewhere between perfecting this art and posting pictures, I forgot that what's inside this body is older than time itself.

My soul has been travelling for eons, and this body is truly a mere vessel. And the human body ages, changes, and evolves. And I still struggle to accept it, to show it for what it is, to thank it for creating human life.

Being well into my 40's feels scary. Somewhere between the reluctance to accept it and the reality of what it is, a sense of "what if" is slowly emerging.

Maybe now I am grown up enough to use the sentence "I'm old enough to know better". And it didn't really have to take four decades to stand in my own power, because age has nothing to do with it.

Maybe some of us just take a bit longer to appreciate that.

And maybe, just maybe, that deserves grace.

It doesn't matter how sad you are,
how "out of sorts" you feel,
I will hold space for all the parts of you
that need love.

I will hold them all until
you can hold yourself again.
I will create a safe haven
where you can cry as much
as you need.

But make no mistake:
no matter how much you think
your light is out,
no matter how much you feel you
have nothing left to give anymore,

you still light my world
the moment you are
next to me.

HOLD ON

Between silver and gold

You can only ever meet people where they are and to the degree of their healing.

They might want to love you and still not have the capabilities of doing so in the way you need and deserve.

Walking away is the most underrated act of self love and, ultimately, compassion. For both of you.

You cannot fix them.

Giving them the answers will deprive them of the growth that comes from their own journey:
their own pain, their own healing.
And if you are not part of it, so be it.

Don't force yourself to stay on a road that wasn't built for you.

LET GO

There's fear in letting go.
Fear of what you might feel.
Fear of what you might not feel.

There's pressure in letting go,
as you let go of what's familiar
and are forced to face the unknown.

There are unanswered questions
that could possibly forever remain unanswered.

There's a rediscovery, an unlearning, a new sense
of self that needs to be born.

And that's scary,
because we always gravitate toward the familiar,
even if it's painful.

But the truth is, beautiful one, what's waiting
for you is standing behind the very same
door you are refusing to close.

ANXIETY CARRIES MESSAGES

I'm starting to sit with my Anxiety,
to really hear what she has to say.
She often nudges me,
"This feels wrong; maybe it's time to step away."

When I ignore her whispers,
my whole being feels it
the tightness in my chest,
the restless thoughts swirling.

It takes a certain bravery to listen,
to acknowledge the weight of her words
without letting them consume me.
I'm learning to give myself grace,
to take a moment, to breathe.

I can honor her concerns
without surrendering to every anxious thought,
even when the world insists,
"Just keep going; it's all fine."

I'll trust my own instinct,
seeking balance through the noise.
In this dance with uncertainty,
I reclaim my voice,
choosing to stand firm,
to embrace my truth,
and to navigate my own path forward,
<u>fear and all</u>.

GROWING PAINS

We are always different versions of ourselves. As we grow and evolve, we say goodbye to the old versions. And that is a grieving process in itself. To recognise that we are no longer that version who would accept less than we deserve or that version who would put everyone else's needs before us.

It's difficult to fully move forward, and we always tend to go back to the most familiar ache.

Let's give ourselves permission to change. To evolve. To take with us the lessons and transform the pain into wisdom.

To fly to where we were always meant to.

Listen to what's not said

Life will always be challenging in one way or another.
Love is the biggest mystery, and yet, it's the life force that
moves us all.
The key is to find someone we match energetically with:
someone who's a soft landing, someone with whom we can
rest when life gets overwhelming.

When we feel depleted, it often comes from spending
too much energy trying to match our partner. We vibrate
at higher frequency and we sometimes lower our own to
meet the shortfall.
The result is disappointment and depletion.

Listen carefully.
Listen with your intuition.

Align with your true energy.
It always knows the way.

Believe

"*Believe in yourself*" is not just a catchphrase.
It is a spell you cast upon yourself.
It is your way to say to the Universe:
"*I am ready.*"
It is your invitation
to take your rightful place in this world.

Are you ready?

BALANCE

Grieving the living is more difficult:
their departure was a choice.
But the truth is:
sometimes we are the shipwreck
and - sometimes - we are the storm.
May you find comfort in the knowledge that
not all waves belong to the sea.

AFFIRMATIONS TO THE UNIVERSE

I am grateful to the Universe and my ancestors for
paving the path to wholeness.

I am blessed to have received the life lessons that
fostered my growth,

grateful for the pain I endured to learn
the wisdom I needed.

I am glad to be where I am in life.
I am excited about the future.

My vibrations are high and pure; they come from a
place of love and acceptance

of everything that has been,

everything that is,

everything that will be.

Faith

The day will come when you'll feel like
you have no more faith,
nothing left to say,
nothing more to give.

Tears will sink down your cheeks
and you will just feel like
abandoning ship.

The waves of the sea of grief seem way too high,
in that moment, my love,
please don't hide.

Cry if you must,
scream at the sky until your lungs burst.
Then look inwards:

you are the safest place you can trust.

Many stories, many lives

I have many stories to tell, so sometimes I feel overwhelmed. From my middle aged wisdom that grows every day into more patience, more acceptance, more gratitude.

I have been dealt so many bad cards (I used to think). "I have been unlucky in love", was my narrative. "I'll never amount to anything", was the silent, running whisper.

I've always felt restless, anxious, out of place, out of sorts. I've been wondering where "my people" were, from a very young age. I confused my intuition for anxiety. All the times I didn't listen to it, my body reacted and I just suppressed it.

Being no longer married felt like an unfamiliar land with no branches to hold on to. Everything I've always wanted wasn't there anymore. The idea of the family I was brought up with no longer was. It takes courage to break away from something that no longer serves us, and even more courage to accept that it was exactly what was meant for us. But I know now that the lessons there would lead me to the most fulfilling life I've ever dreamed of.

You see, fulfilment has always had a different connotation for me:

I used to think it was "success", money, recognition. But everytime I achieved some of it, I felt even *less* fulfilled. The answer was always in understanding what my soul was calling me to do. I don't believe our destiny is decided by someone foreign; I think we decide ourselves before we come on Earth.

And the quest, the journey, the mission is on *remembering* it. And when we do, everything feels calm, everything feels like it makes sense. That's the true fulfilment, the notion that we have finally understood our path and what we came here to do, so we can build the road to get there.

Some roads are longer and have many preparatory steps, bends, and hills to climb. Every step, every disappointment, every tear, every "I can't do this" had something to teach me.

I'm not saying it's been easy, it's been incredibly hard.

But no, I haven't been dealt bad cards. I've been dealt exactly the cards that I needed in order to grow. I've not been unlucky in love. I've been shown what I didn't want and what I was actually worth.

What a gift.

What if I told you that, in this life, the currency is Happiness?

Would you work as hard to get rich?

You don't need to work to earn love

And hear me out:

I don't mean we don't need to put work into a relationship, as it is always a work in progress.

But this is only possible when love is reciprocal and shown through intention and consistency.

Chasing love, seeking external validation, and consuming yourself is not what love is about.

Choose empowered solitude over hollow company.

Don't abandon yourself in the quest of earning love, because love should not and must not be earned.

Trust is earned, respect is non-negotiable, and relationships are built over time.

We are wonderful as we are, and when someone doesn't see this, it's okay.

Truly. But it will never mean that we need to compromise who we are, abandon ourselves, and accept breadcrumbs in the name of a false narrative that people dare to call love.

I refuse to do so.

And that, my friends, that is what protecting our peace means.

That is what living with integrity means.

No one knows you better than you do

No one has more influence on you than you do, and that's how it should be.

When you master your own relationship with yourself, you belong to your own heart. Truly and lovingly. And that's when you can land softly in the most magnificent love for someone else. In the sacred space of our own individuality, which consciously makes space for the other.

It's a choice, one made with love and for love.

Breaking the cycle of toxic relationships begins with the choice of reclaiming ourselves and feeling safe in our own body, our own breath, our own love.

When love comes

When the love of your life arrives,
it may unfold with quiet grace,
a subtle whisper rather than a grand parade.
No fanfare, no soaring Disney ballad,
no proclamations from the rooftops.

It will sneak in a moment of chaos and ground you

    - a gentle anchor in the storm -

and for the first time, you'll feel like
you can lean in rather than holding on.

When the love of your life arrives,
you will find yourself smiling at a new weirdness
that you won't find weird.
You'll breathe freely, at last,
safe in your truest self.

Their energy will embrace yours,
your nervous system will feel calm,
a sense of peace will surround you.
Sleep will come easily; no butterflies
will keep you awake at night.

There won't be chaos around them,
their intentions will be crystal clear
and their actions will match their words.

At first, their difference may guard your heart,
and if this stirs confusion,
it's merely a sign to hold on tight.

When the love of your life arrives,
you may not recognize it at once,
and that's precisely how it's meant to be.

Be You

Be your authentic, beautiful self.
Unveil your soul; allow it to shine brightly in the tapestry
of your existence.

Everything will follow,
like stars aligning in the night sky,
drawing constellations of your dreams.

Even if that means losing people along the journey,
understand that not all are meant to walk
every path with you.

Trust in your journey, for it is uniquely yours:
trials and triumphs, woven with threads of authenticity.

Be you, *unapologetically*,

and let the universe conspire
to unfold the story
that only you can tell.

MADE FOR THE WILD

I was made for the wild, for freedom.
Away from schemes and conventions,
lover of everything dark and mysterious,
blossoming in everything soft and gentle.

And as a free spirit, here's the truth:
you cannot chain a free spirit
but you need to love them hard,
for exactly who they are;
so fragile that all they want to do is fly away,
so strong that their love will be
the most beautiful light the world has ever seen,
so true and authentic that being loved by them
will feel like a r e v o l u t i o n.

Don't settle

It's easy to settle, to stay in the "this is good enough" zone,
    to choose someone out of fear of being alone,
        to accept breadcrumbs and dim your light just

because it is casting shadows
    on those who are not worthy of you.

So wait a week longer,
    a month longer,
        a year longer if you need to.

The right person will cherish you,
    be your biggest fan, and listen to every worry,
        every doubt, every "I can't do this".

They will stay until your heart is calm again,
    and full with all the love you so deserve.

Hand in hand,
    heart to heart,
        step by step

reflecting your magnificent light
    instead of dimming it.

Wait for a love where you can completely melt into,
    and come out on the other side
        whole.

YOU ARE WORTHY, EXACTLY AS YOU ARE

In all your messiness,
in all your contradictions,
in every winter phase of your life.

You are worthy because you are you.
The entire Universe conspired for you to be here,
that's how important you are.

Please stay.

When you feel stuck and
don't know what to do,
when the weight of the world
crushes you with doubt and
false narratives of what you
should do, or say, or be,
ask yourself: What would love do?

And do just that.

Reclaim Yourself

I know you feel the weight of the world today, *I know*.
I know you feel trapped and are envying the birds flying free.
Let not hope flutter away with the breeze.

Change is inevitable and you can *always* begin again.
You can fly again, and maybe - this time -
to a better place, a new and exciting venture.
Nobody can clip your wings,
not even when they're tucked away behind all your fears.

Rest, recuperate. Give yourself space and time.
And when you're ready, reclaim yourself
and fly again, free of the chains of the past.

ASHES AND FIRE

The truth is I am more ashes than fire,
more bones than flesh,
homesick for the stars,
for a place I've never been
yet calls me from within.

The truth is, nobody really knows
what we are here to do.
I know you feel it too.

What if we could just answer the call,
follow our intuition to see where it leads,
quiet the mind to the truth bending our knees.

To the altar in the space between
salvation and redemption,
may this foreign language be fully understood
by our souls.

On some deep level, maybe we know exactly
where it ends.

THE PEOPLE

Move towards people who look at you in awe, who hold a mirror up to yourself that you've never seen before.

Move towards people that make your soul do a summersault within the divinity of a love that is not conditional to any rule.

Those people that only see the purple aura around you even when you are exhausted by the million chores, raising children, bread, and expectations of yourself.

Move towards people that stay behind to ask you how you are twice, if you have eaten enough, if you got home okay. Towards those who ask if you realise how incredible you are and genuinely wait for an answer.

Move towards the worthy ones, the ones you never ever have to second guess, the ones who take you to see the stars just so you feel closer to home.

Let everyone else go.

A THOUSAND POSSIBILITIES

I searched long and deep inside my head only to find thousands and thousands of pages ripped off books and neatly folded.

Each one represents the story that could have played out, but didn't. They looked like origami, and as I opened my heart,

I gasped at how many there were, piling upon each other.

The deeper I looked, the more the pages started to become butterflies and flew away: opening up, releasing, healing.

It's okay if those stories were not meant to be;

I don't need to keep those possibilities inside me.

I can let go now, I can make space for the new ones that - this time - won't get stuck in the chambers of my heart and, instead, *bring light to a new future.*

To love me

Check your ego at the door,
kiss me with that tenderness that makes me ache.

Weave every one of my last hopes back to gold,
open the curtains and show me how the sunrise
casts the shadows away.

Count my bones with your fingers as my hair falls perfectly
between the silk pillowcase and the depth of your soul.

Give me the love you can't name,
the one that leaves us breathless with every exhale,
overwhelmed by how right it feels.

Give me a lavender field of peace and yearning.
Give me e v e r y t h i n g.

Everything that money can't buy.

It wasn't love

It had nothing to do with love.
Your heart was broken, your heart was shattered,
your ego bruised.
Love wasn't the problem, it was a person who hurt you.
Someone who couldn't quite meet you where you were.

It was a person that broke your heart, not love.
Love doesn't hurt: love is beautiful, healing, and pure.

Don't give up on love because someone couldn't handle
your magnificence.

Don't give up on love.

Wonderfully You

You are not damaged;

you are scarred.

You are not broken;

you are healing.

You are not "too much".

You are everything

this world needs

more

of.

In the quiet of the morning

In the quiet of the morning, I found the safety of my breath, the comfort of waking up early and not feeling tired.

The silent humming within that speaks of gratitude and compassion in a renewed sense of hope.

In the quiet of the morning I found answers to questions posed aeons ago, flowing like a river through my veins.

Listening to the silence, I could make sense of each atom of soundless presence, like a book, only I could read its invisible ink,

Like a page written only for me in an ancient language that the quiet of the morning gave me the key to.

Answers always arrive in the most unexpected ways.

Trust in the u n f o l d i n g.

Scars

It is difficult to count how many scars life has already caused, but maybe I don't need to; I feel them all. They are part of me.

Today I decided to shine a light under each one of them, and what a sight unfolded before my eyes.

All the lights lit up at once, in the darkness and before my eyes a map of a constellation appeared. My own universe of wisdom, love, hard-earned lessons, and tears that birthed compassion.

Each scar lit up in such a way that I couldn't be angry anymore. I felt gratitude, I felt joy, I felt I could finally let go of that pain and embrace the beauty of what I saw.

A woman who stands in her power, not ashamed of her vulnerability, is a woman who IS ready to take her rightful place in this world.

A woman forged in fire.

NEW LOVE

I wish you a love that wants you with messy hair
and stains on your shirt when the kids are eating
and playing with their food.

I wish you a love that takes its time to reveal itself
and doesn't rush in, because to say "I love you"
will mean I love all of you.

I wish you a love that builds you a home for your heart
that won't be shaken by any storm.

I wish you a love that reads your silences
like red capital letters on a billboard
and knows exactly how to hold you.

I wish you a love that makes you feel
calm, secure, loved, excited:
safe in the highest of heights,
breathless in the steadiest of breaths.

THE ROAD

The road to healing has more "No" than "Yes".
More "*What's going on?*" and less
"*Why has this happened to me?*"

Less "I" and more "We".

Recognising the shadows as something we are called to soften,
with the infinite light we are made of
that we don't always see.

IF LOVE WERE A SHAPE, WHAT WOULD IT BE?

An infinity symbol,
smooth and predictable,
asymmetrical emotions,
a multifaceted gem,

the same object seen
from different perspectives
like a vase between us.
We each see only one side,

yet spend our lives
trying to glimpse the other.
So, when you ask me what love is,
I can only say:

 "It's the attempt to see the other side."

The answer must be the attempt.

Your soul has a voice

Stay still and quiet;
let it come to you.
Feel your body, your muscles,
your hair, your feet on the ground.
Feel the energy moving in
and through your body.
Listen calmly;
your soul has a voice:
a voice that is loudest
in total silence.

WHERE LOVE FLOWS FREELY

Go where there's flow.
I don't mean going with the flow;
I mean go where there's no resistance.

Go where you're welcomed and your energy cherished.
Go where there's nothing to prove.
Go where love flows easily and in sync with your heart.

Be choosy, be demanding in how your energy is reciprocated.
Go where adoration is the first course and not the main meal,
as anything less is not worth disturbing your peace.

Go where you feel that time stops.
Go with long kisses and eye conversations.
Go where plans are dreams that you can't wait to happen.

Go where you can say at night
"I have everything my heart desires".

Go there and *stay*.

Yes you can.

Yes, YOU can!
You have done it before and you can do it again.
It hurts because you thought they were the answer.
But a person can never be the whole answer to any
question.

It takes energy and alignment,
and the universe removes all that is not aligned with us.
I know you don't want to hear it.
I've been there. I see you.
I know you're hurting.

But you can and will get through this.

YES, YOU CAN

A WISH

And if I had only one wish, I'd spend it on you: I'd ask
for your heart to be so full of light that you
dance in the middle of the kitchen,
singing at the top of your lungs.

If I had only one wish, I'd ask that you could taste the
last bite of a summer strawberry as if it were
sacred nectar; I'd ask for all your senses to be
so heightened that you feel you are

in a room of heaven on earth. If I had only one wish, I'd
ask for all your insecurities to leave the room in a
grand farewell party where all the spectators
rejoice at the big exit. If I had only one wish,

I'd spend it on you so you could live your life in love,
compassion, and truth, in all the things made of
everything that money can't buy. If I had one
wish, I'd ask for your happiness to be so

infectious that your smile can and will save the world. If
I had only one wish, I'd ask for you to believe in
yourself, because there is nothing more magical
than conquering your own magnificence.

Because, believe me, you are:
You are absolutely magnificent.

Some questions are not revealed
until the answers arrive.

Just wait

.

Learning to Embrace the Now

One of the hardest lessons was learning to embrace the present: accepting things as they are, especially in heartbreak's shadow.

Heartbreak has been a lifelong companion. Clinging to memories of hurt, wishing words unsaid, replaying final moments, rewriting stories in my mind— a way to hold onto grief, to stay close to those who left.

With time, I've learned to see differently. As pain fades from body, soul, and mind, a new reality dawns.

It wasn't happening to me, but for me— to teach me, to help me evolve, to remind me never to settle for less.

To trust myself, to love myself wholly, not in fragments.

This is the only way to show the universe I've learned to love myself a little bit more.

There is another way to love, and I'm discovering it now. A love without second-guessing, without compromising who I am.

A love where I feel beautiful and powerful, a love that lets me look back and say:

I get it. I get it, universe. *Thank you.*

Embracing Shadows

Normalise feeling blue, out of sorts, weary.
Let's accept we are beings of light and shadow.
Happiness isn't constant, nor should it be.

When the world feels too much, let darkness be a friend,
offer it love and compassion,
as it's there to restore our energy.

Turn inward and ride the waves,
embrace the shadows; you'll find growth.
It's a metamorphosis my love:
— no great change comes without discomfort.
So let the darkness teach you its secrets,
like a deep ocean concealing its treasures.
In its profound silence, find the pearls of your own truth,

and emerge transformed,
a beacon of light born from the depths
ready to take on the world.

When you don't feel good enough

It happens, you know?
The waking up feeling not good enough,
not pretty enough,
not thin enough,
not rich enough,
not happy enough.

Where does this word even come from?
It rhymes with "huff" and "puff"
and it sounds more ridiculous
the more I say it.
I wonder if I could re-frame the sentence:

"Today I don't feel puff" instead of
"I don't feel enough"
It's funny I laugh,
I'm not thinking of it in the same way.

Maybe that's the point:
having the ability to laugh at ourselves,
to reframe words and beliefs
when we wake up a different and darker
version of ourselves?

Maybe I can soften the blow,
smile a bit and let it flow,
watch the words twist and play,
from enough to

I love you today.

I say out loud in the mirror:
"I love you".
And for the first time
she smiles back at me,

a silent affirmation
a quiet revelation
and I realise that I am enough.

I have *always* been <u>enough</u>.

Go gentle on yourself

Your inner critic will always find fault;
it's simply fulfilling its role.
Awaken your inner supporter
and pay attention to its voice.
Observe the interplay between the two.

Please, let the inner supporter
have its moment in the sun, too.

THE EXTRAORDINARY ORDINARY

We chase the extraordinary
without stopping to bless the ordinary.

But loving our children -
that's far from ordinary, don't you think?
The chance to love and be loved
by a being you created is e x t r a o r d i n a r y.

Maybe happiness is just this:
finding a smile after a hard day,
hugging yourself tight, saying,
"Look at what you've created;
look how lucky you are to experience this."

I used to chase the extraordinary -
millions of followers, best seller rankings,
and maybe I still do.
But these days, it doesn't hold me hostage
as much as it once did.

I choose to draw energy from the everyday.
I choose to open my eyes and keep them fixed
on what truly matters to me.

Open your eyes my love, open your eyes.

FLY WITH ME, OR NOT

I refuse to live in fear.
I release all doubts and chains;
I'm tired of leaving it all to chance.

I am grabbing life by the horns; I will make it happen:
whatever it is my heart is longing for,
whatever it is my soul is craving.

I don't know how many lives we have,
or if I will remember this one when I enter the next realm.
But when all is said and done, when the chips are down
and the flames are extinguishing,
I want to say "I lived".
To the fullest, with integrity,
true to myself and what I stand for.
I stand with the truth, with love: soft, open, alive.
I want to fly away, free and happy.

You can fly with me for a while, or for longer.
But fly with me, not around me or behind me.
Feel the wind and the freedom, and when you want to rest,
feel free to take a breath.

Just don't look back.

That's progress, that's the journey to happiness.
Fly with me, or not.

I am going anyway.

Untamed Magnificence

Don't make yourself smaller just because they can't hold
your infinite magnificence,
beautiful soul.

The fire inside your wild heart has been burning since the
beginning of time
and it was never meant to be tamed.

Fly,
inspire,
soar,
burn.

Surrender

What if the scariest thing was the stepping stone you
needed to fly?

What if you could re-frame that fear into opportunity?

What if we could just surrender to the
Universe and the journey?

What if you could trust that you are exactly where
you are meant to be?

What if you needed those shadows to wrap around you
like a blanket so you could rest?

What if this stillness was the only progress you needed?

What if in the absence of words, you could finally find
your voice?

Reflections

There is nothing more poetic
than listening to your own reflection
softly whispering:
"You are doing just fine".
Because you are, my friend. You are.

Tenderness that aches

The only love I'll ever settle for Is the one I don't have to
fight for.
I don't care about money, status,
or anything that shines.
I want time,
I want conversations,
I want the raw truth,
I want the "I don't want to kiss you yet"
so we can talk more.

I want laughter that comes easily,
silences that feel like home,
eyes that meet and understand,
a touch that speaks without words.
I want the mundane moments,
the grocery runs and late-night talks,
the quiet mornings and shared dreams.

I want the honesty that cuts through the noise,
the vulnerability that brings us closer,
the comfort in simply being,
without pretence, without masks.
I want the kind of love
that grows in the cracks of everyday life,
that finds beauty in the ordinary,
and strength in the storms.

I want a love that's patient,
that doesn't rush or force,
but unfolds naturally,
with grace and mutual respect.

The only love I'll ever settle for
is the one that feels like coming home,
where my heart can rest easy,
and my soul can be free.
I want a love that's real,
that's tender and kind,
a love that nourishes,
a love that's mine.

The bird that flew away

And when they ask you about me,
how I chose to live my life,
why I decided to let go of negativity,
tell them I was the bird who
                    f l e w
                              a w a y.

Tell them my secrets were too big for
their small ears.
Tell them my heart swelled outside
of my tiny ribcage.
Tell them the fire didn't tame me.

Tell them,
I was the fire
              itself.

BUTTERFLIES

Butterflies are not always
a sign of love and connection.
Seek the one that makes your heart
feel calm and at peace,
and you might just find
your home.

Sadness is with Me

Sadness is with me, if you're looking for her.
She arrived quietly, almost unexpectedly, carrying heavy bags.
I really thought she'd pack lightly, just a small suitcase of memories,
but no, her load is weighty,
filled with echoes of yesterdays and unspoken words.

She always has this habit of showing up when I need to do other things,
interrupting my plans with her sombre presence.
I think I will let her be for a while, lean into me,
her head resting softly on my shoulder.
I'll sit with her in this shared silence,
acknowledging her existence without rushing her away.

I'll tell Joy we are on our way,
send a whisper into the wind,
a promise that we'll be together soon.

ON CHRISTMAS DAY

Merry Christmas to the ones who have their hearts full and for those who have their hearts broken. Whichever stage you are at please know I am proud of you. If all you did today was just to get out of bed, or if you're busy with a million preparations for Christmas.

This time can be so hard for many, so whether you celebrate it or not, don't forget how far you've come this year.

Rest, recuperate and celebrate yourself for all you've done and for the days you didn't want to carry on, but did. For the endless chores and homework with the children, for the days you were too tired but went out anyway to celebrate your friend's birthday. For making your house a home and pouring love from an empty cup. For never failing to show up.

I am proud of you. And I want you to be, too.

Merry Christmas to the dreamers, to the hopeless romantics, to the visionaries. Never forget how much love this world needs from you as you raise the vibrations of this earth. Please keep going and don't let heartbreak turn you cold.

Merry Christmas to the mums and parents who keep the spirit of Christmas alive for their children amidst a wounded world.

Merry Christmas to those of you who are grieving the loss of a loved one or are experiencing their first holiday without one. Remember they are with you, they reside in your heart amongst all the love that makes grief impossible to sustain. There is love, there always was, and there always will be.

Merry Christmas to the ones that don't celebrate and just want to spend the next 3 days in bed. I'll virtually extend my blanket of love to keep you warm

Whatever you do, please know you are loved.

You are very much loved indeed.

New Year's Eve

I don't wish you to have a new resolution tonight;
I wish you the strength to check in with yourself every week.

I don't wish you to be a new you tonight;
I wish you'd be kinder to yourself every day of the year.

I wish you'd see how amazing you already are, count your successes today,
and do exactly the same every day to come.

I wish we could all wish each other Happy New Month every 5 weeks and welcome our struggles as much as we welcome our joys and see beauty in the journey.

I wish we could reflect on our journey, not just at the end of the year, but every night as we close our eyes and exhale the day. May we stop, reflect, and love ourselves for who we really are.

I wish we would say to ourselves 'I am proud of you'. Today. Tomorrow. Next month. Next year.

Happy New Day. Happy New Month. Happy New Year.

Learn to trust your intuition,
Learn to trust your own answers.
You are your greatest teacher

CLOSE THE DOOR

Close the door,
open the windows,
burn some sage.

Let the music beat
in sync with your heart.

Slow down.

Breathe,
breathe some more,
let the tears cleanse your soul.

Take stock;
sometimes stillness
is the only progress
we need.

Magic

I believe in magic,
in the magic of listening to one another:
not just hearing the words, but understanding them.
In those moments when nothing really makes sense,
when screaming would be easier,
where running away feels like the only option.
Magic is found in stillness.

Breathe,
         listen,
                  repeat.

Fire

The fire in you
was never meant
to be tamed.
Those flames are meant
to light the world.

You are a "Yes"

You are an answer,
not a question.
You are a certainty,
not a doubt.
Do you hear me?
You are a
"Yes"
    not a
        "Maybe".

Poets

I am a rebel child,
a complacent adult,
an anxious woman.

I no longer break my own heart to save others.

There is another way:
another way to love,
another way to help,
another way to be.

I've started to look for the path
where I can help without hurting
through energy, through love.

I am fascinated by the Universe,
by all the invisible forces that drive us on:
homesick for the stars,
yearning for silence and quiet within.

I feel drawn by Egypt, the goddesses,
and a sense of order.
The higher the energy, the higher the order.

I am a lover of cats,
mother of daughters,
divine feminine energy
trapped in a tiny body.

A vessel of truth for others:

awakening activator through love,
through ancient ancestral knowledge,
unwanted in physical form
yet called to bring light and wisdom.

All I have are my words.
I am my words.
I am more. I need to do more.

I am a medicine woman,
a starseed from Sirios,
destined for greatness.

I am divine,
I am a guide
I am a teacher.

I am a poet.

IN THIS HOUSE

In this house, we have lots of brushes and can never find
hair bobbles.
We stretch out on Sundays like cats and never rush.
We love the slowness of the weekend mornings - (even the
cats wake up before we do).

In this house, we are painters and musicians and poets:
we use words, colours and notes
to tell our version of the truth.

We are loud, messy, and wonderfully gentle
and we don't know how not to say hello
without a smile.

We wait for the owls to let us know it is safe to be out
and we never tell lies to each other.
In this house we are growing up, growing old, growing happy.

We are learning new skills, reframing old ones, practising
our roars
for a world that is patiently waiting
for a grand debut.

In this house, we gather around the kitchen table
and give a name to the cooker.
We laugh as we make biscuits and shape them like hearts.

In this house, we know that the truth is more real
around the kitchen table
where you both look at me like the steadiest of rocks.

I clutch my kitchen apron, and I realise
that in your growth, I find my purpose.
I hope my love will always be enough.

In this house, we are all doing our best -
you both call me home

I call you l i f e.

OVER-LOVE

So you overthink.
So you overtalk.
So you overfeel.
So you overlove.
I think that is absolutely
beautiful.

DO MORE

If you want more love,
give more love.
If you want to be heard,
do more listening.
If you seek connection,
connect more deeply.
If you want to feel understood,
offer understanding.
Do more.
Give more.
Do what you need more of,
and watch the energy shift.
See how kindness returns to you,
tenfold.
In giving, you find the love you seek,
and the world sends it back.
It always sends it back.

BREATHE

Every smile that we manage to do is a blessing,
and every tear is necessary for our growth.
The right decision is the one that comes without drama
and only a sense of *peace*.
It might be that it's not happening soon though...
This only means that we are not ready yet
or that the timing is not on our side,
so we just need to breathe through this bad day
and give our brain a much-needed break.
There is always tomorrow.
There is *always* tomorrow.

THE DIAMOND OF THE SOUL

A diamond is made of many facets, each one shining differently as light moves through it. Though the diamond itself remains still, it is constantly challenged by the shifting light. Our soul is much like a diamond, full of facets, each representing different aspects of our being. At different times in our lives, different facets will shine the brightest, while others may remain dusty and in need of polishing.

Throughout our journey, we encounter people who help us polish these facets. Some are fleeting, their purpose fulfilled quickly. I call these "the teachers." They appear, deliver their lesson, and then vanish, having given us what we needed at that moment.

Others stay longer, helping us polish more stubborn, neglected facets. These are "the saviours," the ones who lift us up and remind us of the hidden beauty within ourselves. They help us see that what we once thought was a piece of old, broken metal is actually a part of our radiant diamond.

Then there are those who help us reflect the light already within us. These are "the keepers." They are the companions we meet time and time again across lifetimes. Their energy balances us, and they arrive after many journeys, when the foundations have been laid by the teachers and saviours. The keepers show us how to shine our own light from within, bringing us peace.

In between each journey, as one facet starts to reflect its intended light, we often find ourselves restless, ready to work on the next facet. Love, tenderness, friendship, family, work, passion, trust, and honesty are just some of the facets we polish throughout our lives. Each person we meet plays a role in this process, whether we realize it or not.

Some come and go: sometimes tragically, sometimes by choice, and sometimes inexplicably. Others remain. The duration of their presence depends on their role, and though we may not always understand their purpose until the end, I believe everything happens for a reason. Life is beautifully orchestrated, and that's why I don't push for things. I've been a teacher, a saviour, and a keeper for others, and I move through life with curiosity and an open mind.

Now, when I feel restless, I understand it's because I'm polishing a new facet of my diamond. If it's a teacher helping me, they will be with me for a short while. If it's a saviour, they will stay longer. As for the keepers, their presence is a profound mystery. I don't believe we have just one keeper in life, but a few, each arriving at different times to help us polish the most important facets. When we recognize them, we must hold on to them.

When keepers find each other, we have it all. These relationships, where both individuals are keepers for one another, are the soulmates of life. We are all teachers, saviours, and keepers, finding each other at the right times in this wonderful journey.

So, I do not worry about or force anything. I embrace each phase. When I get hurt, I know it's because I've been scratching the diamond too hard instead of polishing it with care. Let the light shine always. Life is infinitely beautiful, and we are fortunate to learn from it. Even through pain and disappointment, I trust that it is just the final polish before a new light shines again.

Open your heart
to the one
you can safely
be silent with.

Do not give up

It's okay to feel scared.
It's okay to feel lost.
It's okay to struggle.
It's okay.
You are okay.
Do not give up.
Trust that your heart will heal;
choose possibility over infeasibility.
Ditch logic, ditch the odds,
and hold on to
hope.

Shortfalls

You only accept the love you *think* you deserve.
Do not lower your value to match someone else's shortfalls.
Never dim your light to absorb another's shadow.

Trust that the Universe has plans for you,
greater than you can imagine,
and know that you hold the key to all its secrets.

For you are e n o u g h, in every way,
in every breath,
in every heartbeat,
in every atom of every star
in every galaxy.

A masterpiece, come what may.

You come from the stars,
so aim for home.
What you seek
is seeking You
in return.

LET YOUR SOUL REMEMBER

In your darkest moments, remember:
it is just a phase, it will not last forever.
You can do this;
you already have
in all your lifetimes.
Let your soul remember and guide you.

BORN OF LIGHT AND DARKNESS

I was born in just twenty seconds - my late mother used to say I was always in a rush. To live, to love, to be a wife, a mother, a career woman.

But being a poet? That wasn't something I rushed into, because you can't hurry into what you've always been.

Deep down, I've always felt like I was late to something important. Like there was a bigger purpose waiting for me - to add my voice, to offer courage, comfort, maybe even light. And so, I write, not to compete, but to let you know that you are not alone.

I'm not here to offer a quick fix, but to sit with you when life feels too heavy. Because I know that when it's dark, it's pitch black. And I'll be there, sitting with you in the shadows, until the light comes again.

I was born in twenty seconds, with a soul that feels like it came from another galaxy - in a hurry to get here.

And if it's true that I come from the stars, I don't just want to shine my light on you. I want to help you to find your own, too.

I was born in just twenty seconds.

HOPE

And one day, we will finally understand
and make sense of it all.
Until then, all we can do
is to hold on
to
Hope.

To be a mother

You sit at my dressing table amongst bottles of perfume and makeup you don't yet know how to use. All I hear is the noise of the opening and closing of the hair straightener that you are using to fix your curly hair that you have started not to like; your young fingers learn how not to burn yourself in the name of a new concept of beauty that goes beyond the eyes of a mother.

And a gnawing feeling in the pit of my stomach reminds me that you are no longer a baby.

And I wonder how much less you need me now and, somehow, how much more you need me for everything that you don't want to ask me out loud. I stare at you silently, as my role is now to look after you in the background of a new identity forming that it is still so delicate.

Long gone are the days when you wouldn't leave my side when I was putting makeup on before work, hoping you wouldn't cry as I stepped out of the door. And I don't know if I'm more nostalgic for the days when you needed me like oxygen or for the ones you actively choose to sit with me.

All I know is that I drink you in like golden sunshine for all the times I'll still get to see you daily before you'll be ready to leave the nest, and all I can think about is what an honour it is to be a mother. What an honour it is to pave your path and see you growing into a wise and strong young woman.

What an honour it is to teach you the power of kindness and compassion.

What an honour it is to learn from you that I'm doing a good job when you hug me out of the blue and you tell me you love me.

You ask me why do I have tears in my eyes and all I can say is:

What an honour it is

to be YOUR mother.

The answer

The answer is always somewhere not too far:
in the smile of a stranger,
in a quote you find by chance,
in the unexpected compassion of a someone new,
in a poignant question from a child.
The universe *always* works its magic.
We just have to be ready to listen.

Please breathe,
and listen.

For poets and artists

It will come back, you know?

The spark, the creativity, the genius, the pen flowing on its own.
Poets write the most when hurt,
when only the page can listen to ghosts.
Our job is to notice, to observe, to immortalise.

But, oh, how Joy deserves it though,
to be cherished.
So write about how your mouth forgot to smile,
but Joy reminded it how to lift at its corners.

Write about how your heart is no longer as heavy,
how watermelon suddenly tastes so much better
when the bite follows a kiss.

It will come back, you know?

It's okay to be happy, it's okay to pause to feel it all
and shut down the world.
If it's true for sadness, it has to be even more for Joy.

It will come back, you know?

PERMISSION TO CHANGE

Give yourself permission:
to change,
to evolve,
to become a different version of you.
Honour the old you;
she took you right to where you are now.
Allow your wings to open up
and fly to where you were
always meant to.

Be Ready

Maybe it takes time because you have to be ready for it. And I don't mean being ready to actually do what you are dreaming of, but being ready to believe that you are worthy of r e c e i v i n g it. When you start believing, in your bones, in every atom of your every cell, that's when the Universe makes magic happen.

When you finally decide that you deserve unconditional love, that you are worth so much more than the half-hearted, uncertain, "let's see how it goes" kind of love, the Universe will open the door for the right person to come in. With them, you won't feel breathless. Instead, you will feel like you have an extra pair of lungs. Your heart won't pound in your chest. You will experience a level of bliss that makes you wonder what dreams are even made of—still as a lake, calm as a swan, pure as the snow.

When you finally decide that you are ready to be seen and accepted by the world, when you accept that your voice deserves to be heard, the Universe will conspire to make it happen. Because your voice needs to be heard: across mountains, through deserts and rivers, reaching every last soul who needs to know how wonderful they are.

So go on and take up s p a c e. Be loud, be present, be unique. Say what you need to say, then say it again. And again.

In every form, in every shape, in every universe. Don't let numbers and mundane things question the importance of what you're saying. Do it for free, do it with hope, do it with love.

Keep going, even when you feel like you're ready to quit. That's often when the biggest changes happen.

Take space, be loud, be present, be unique. Say what you need to say, then say it again.

And again.

   And again.

       And again.

Choose to place hope where once there was fear.

The quiet wisdom

I don't have many words today,
or yesterday, or the day before.
I'm learning to breathe in the day
and appreciate it for what it is.

I don't have many words to express
how I'm content in my own company,
so much so that it feels unnerving.
How have I never learned this before?
I think I would have spared myself
a lot of heartbreak.

I don't have many words today
to express how the mirror reflects
an image I don't recognize
because it's not in pieces.

There isn't a single person I can attribute this to.
I don't have enough poetry
to describe the happiness
of making breakfast and eating it at 6:45 a.m.
before my daughter leaves for school,
feeling like I have a purpose.

It doesn't really matter If my books
don't reach millions.
So many other poets
say what I want to say
in a way that seems *so much better.*
And a thought dawns on me:

What if the secret of true happiness is exactly this?
Being happy for other people's successes,
being brave enough to be a mother
and fully embrace what that means,
being strong enough to say "not today"
and walk away from toxicity.

What if the wisdom we seek
is hidden within everyday moments,
in the quiet peace that comes
from embracing life as it is?

Aren't you tired yet?

Aren't you tired yet:
of this life full of lies and doubts,
being second-guessed and taken for granted?

Aren't you tired yet;
of putting a mask on and faking a smile
when all you want to do is to crumble?

Aren't you tired yet:
of saying "Yes, I'll work on it" when
the only thing you should be working on
is enforcing your own boundaries?

Saying "No" does not require apologies.
Being you, and being proud of who you are
does not require any validation.

Tell me, aren't you tired yet:
of trying to fit into a world of chaos,
of listening to what people say you should be?

Because your heart has already known grief,
loss, and betrayal, and it is now your time to shine.

Step out of the shadows and embrace who you are,
because you are wonderful and everything
this world needs more of.

Tell me:
aren't you tired yet of not believing any of this?

EMPTY FOR ALL THE RIGHT REASONS

And if you have to feel empty,
feel empty for all the right reasons.

Like the clouds after a storm,
like the moon after her full season.

There is a time for everything;
let rest be an important one.

Cherish what has been,
bask in the light that has come.

Celebrate the storm that has finally gone away.

In the safety of new arms,
amongst closed doors,

Watching a new dawn
in silence,
            in something resembling love.

LOOK AHEAD

Maybe it's time to put the weapons down.
Maybe it's time to cherish what was instead of chasing it back.
Futures that never came need to be grieved,
to be missed in all their magnificence that never manifested.

Dust yourself off, dry the tears, the time is now to stand tall.
The future is just ahead of you, within hands' reach, in all
its unknown glory.
Maybe it's time to be courageous enough to say goodbye,
to stop the mind from living in a fantasy that it has created...

Maybe it's time to live in the now.

The present moment is all we have.

The Publisher

The publisher asked me how my book was different from the others in my niche, and I thought of a million reasons... then went down to hundreds, then tens...then maybe one or two.

Why do I need to be different to spread my word? Why can't we work together, and lift each other up instead of using separation as a reason to define our worth?

Why can't I say: here's my contribution to some new concepts that are being discussed, and explored, that are etched in love, compassion, energy, and a beautiful idea of union instead of separation?

To say that my book is so different would mean that I am different from you, which means you and I are separate, which means I am better than you. Which means my ego is leading the way instead of my soul. And none of this is true.

I hope my book is similar to the words of my teachers, to the wisdom of my inspirations. I hope my words will sit alongside theirs to co-create a shared new consciousness that the world is starting to embrace and move towards.

I am joining like-minded souls who are also contributing their voices to a collective chorus.

We are not competing; we are harmonising.

So, when the publisher asked for uniqueness, I realised my book wasn't about being different; it was about being part of something greater.

It was about connection, not distinction.

The publisher didn't publish my book.

I did it anyway.

I HOPE YOU KNOW

When the sun sets, it won't matter what job you had
or how much you earned.
What will matter is how people remember you:

for your compassion and understanding,
for kissing your kids goodnight,
for tiptoeing out of their room.

What will matter is how you never gave up
when life threw you stones,
how you smiled for everyone and helped
even when you couldn't help yourself.

Days are numbered, that's for sure,
but memories are immortal.
Teachings and words live on for generations.

Let compassion be your legacy.
Let the world remember you for your love,
for embracing your journey,
for guiding others through the darkest nights.

For making mistakes but always getting back up,
for never letting fear stay for too long.

Let love be what they remember.

Let it be love.

Thank you for spending time reading my words, I can't think of a more humbling experience than to have someone freely giving me their time.

I hope you have taken something you needed from these pages, and that these words have resonated, healed, and helped you as much as they have helped me putting them on paper. I hope you found your message.

If you have followed me for a while and read my previous books you will recognise some of the poems which I have decided to incorporate in this brand-new book alongside new ones.

Those are pieces that have deeply resonated with my audience in the years; I wanted to write a book that would be just about empowerment, healing, hope, and the beauty of lessons. How pain can always be transformed into wisdom, no matter how dark the skies are.

I wanted to write a book that could be a virtual friend to turn to when needed.

I hope I did just that and I hope you know, by now, how important you are in this Universe.

I believe in the power of community, in the infinite wonderful strength of common humanity. And it starts with gratitude, it always starts with gratitude.

So thank You, whoever you are, wherever you are right now reading these words, I am grateful for You.

If you have enjoyed this book, please do consider leaving a review and/or suggesting it to someone you love. I would like that very much.

Barbara

Acknowledgments

Thank you to my advanced reader group and all the Instagram poetry community for your support and giving my voice a place: I genuinely don't think I'd be here today without you.

There are no coincidences in the world, indeed, so a special thank you goes to Stephen Sainato whose work I connect with deeply at a soul level: thank you for reminding me why I do what I do; the world is a better place with people like you in it.

A special thank you to Dene Logan, incredible woman and talented author, for giving me her time and wonderful review of this book ahead of time.

Thank you, Emmanuel, for being by my side for every project, this is the 5th book you have brought to life from a word file, and I am never in less awe of your talent, dedication and more importantly the love you have for our family.

My sister Renata, life-coach and rock in every storm, thank you for allowing me to discover who I wanted to be; without you there would never be any books!

To my girls Eli and Erica: thank you for making me feel like a rock star every time someone asks you what your mum does for a living.

Finally, a thank you to my mum in heaven: words carry frequency, and frequency is energy, and I want to believe there is a part of her that can read this so thank you for giving me my words so I could share them with the world. *Look mum, look what I have done.*

About the Author

Barbara Gianquitto is a poet, writer, and author of the best-selling poetry collections 4:04am Thoughts, Awakening of the Heart, and Mirrors of Time. Named one of the top 10 authors to watch in 2023, Barbara's work delves into themes of love, heartbreak, self-discovery, and healing. With her soft, unique voice, she has attracted over 90,000 readers worldwide via social media and has been featured on BBC national radio.

Barbara holds a BA Hons degree in Communication and Psychology and is also a certified Neuro-Linguistic Programming (NLP) practitioner and coach. Her passion for language and communication drives her to inspire readers to reflect, heal, and connect with their inner strength.

In addition to her poetry, Barbara is a children's author. Her book Loretta and the Monday Morning Blues helps children understand and validate their emotions, teaching them that it's okay to feel what they feel, and that happiness can be found in the smallest moments.

Originally from Italy, Barbara now lives in the United Kingdom with her family and two cats who think they're dogs. A coffee enthusiast and incurable romantic, she follows the phases of the Moon with fascination.

If you enjoyed I Hope You Know, you will also enjoy:

4:04am Thoughts
Awakening of the Heart
Mirrors of Time

Printed in Great Britain
by Amazon